W9-CFP-556

DATE			

Plant Sculptures

JACK KRAMER

Plant Sculptures

MAKING MINIATURE INDOOR TOPIARIES

photographs by Matthew Barr
drawings by Tom Adams

William Morrow and Company
New York 1978

Library of Congress Cataloging in Publication Data

Kramer, Jack (date)
    Plant sculptures.

    Summary: Discusses how the art of topiary can be performed indoors with house plants and gives instruction for ten projects.
    1. Topiary work—Juvenile literature. 2. Indoor gardening—Juvenile literature. [1. Topiary work. 2. Indoor gardening. 3. Gardening] I. Barr, Matthew. II. Adams, Tom. III. Title.
SB463.K7   635.9′65   78-2524
ISBN 0-688-22144-0
ISBN 0-688-32144-5 lib. bdg.

Printed in the United States of America.
First Edition
1 2 3 4 5 6 7 8 9 10

—

Acknowledgments for Photographs

Clark, 58
Jack Kramer, 15
Scharmer, 10

No book is a single effort; many friends helped and my thanks to them, especially Tom Adams, who did the drawings for this book, and Roy Crafton, who helped to create the plant sculptures.

Contents

Plant Sculptures

outdoor topiary on a grand scale

An Introduction to Plant Sculptures

Making plant sculptures offers an exciting way to garden and craft at the same time. Technically referred to as *topiary,* this popular outdoor gardening art consists of trimming shrubs and trees into large ornamental shapes of geometric designs, animals, or profiles of people. An appealing and easy way to enjoy plant sculptures indoors is to fashion small-scale topiaries.

The miniature, indoor plant sculptures in this book are made by first constructing a decorative wire form in the shape of an animal and then training common houseplants to grow around it. Shaping the wire form and training the plant requires a few ordinary tools and patience. You may have a finished topiary in anywhere from two to six months, depending on the maturity of the plants, how fast they grow, and the number of wires to cover in the form.

But the rewards are well worth the time and effort. Every day the shape you have selected grows in size as the plant does. Whether for the windowsill or table, plant sculptures are fun to make and will give a new and different look to your houseplants.

Basic Equipment and Procedures

MATERIALS AND TOOLS

galvanized wire—14 or 16 gauge
 (or coat-hanger wire)
wire cutter
epoxy ribbon, such as Duro *E·pox·e Ribbon*
string or *Tie-ems* (or plastic ribbons)
sphagnum moss
florist wire
clay pots—10 or 12 inch
work gloves
manicure scissors or paring knife
needlenose pliers
modeling clay or spring-type clothespins

WIRE

Making wire forms is fun, but the wire can be hard to handle. The edges can cut your hands if you are not careful. Always remember to point the sharp ends away from your body, especially your face. In the beginning you should wear gloves until you are more experienced in handling the wire.

The forms for the plant sculptures are made of galvanized wire. To make the animal shapes, use fourteen- or sixteen-gauge wire. Fourteen-gauge wire is flexible and easy to bend by hand, so it is perfect for animal shapes. You can also use coat hangers, taken apart with pliers, for small wire forms.

Surplus stores and some hardware stores and mail-order suppliers sell 100-foot coils of wire, which is enough to make four or five forms. Or you can buy smaller coils of wire at hardware stores. All wire used in the projects can be cut with a wire cutter.

SHAPING WIRE FORMS

Shaping the wire is not difficult. If it kinks in places, you can still use it because the leaves will cover the kinks as the plant grows.

Before beginning a project, practice by making a few basic curves with the wire. To make a smooth curve or a circle, cut a twelve- or eighteen-inch piece of wire from the coil and securely grip one end with the needlenose pliers. Hold the other end of the wire at least twelve inches away from you. Slowly swing around the end that is pointed away from you. With your fingers and thumb, stroke the wire gently and ease it into a curve. Keep practicing with pieces of wire until you can make the curve quickly and smoothly.

To make U shapes, which are used for the ears and tails of animals, hold one end of a piece of wire in your left hand. Bend the wire with the balls of your right thumb and forefinger. With the ball of your thumb, move the wire up and around the top of your forefinger. The U shape may be small or large, depending on the exact shape you want.

All the wire shapes in this book are supported by two straight pieces called "support" wires. These wires, which are attached to the bottom of the form, are then inserted into the soil. *Always be certain these support wires are pushed deep into the soil before continuing work.*

JOINING WIRES

To join two wires, use epoxy ribbon, which is widely available at hardware stores. This ribbon has the consistency of modeling clay and is easy to work with when pressed around joints. When completely dry, the bond is permanent. To use the epoxy material pinch off about one-quarter inch from the ribbon and roll it between your fingers until it is the right consistency (like putty). To secure the wires you want joined, insert the ends in modeling clay or hold them together with spring-type clothespins. Mold the epoxy material around the joint; in two hours you will be able to handle the wires and in twelve hours the joints will be permanently set (almost as hard as steel). For fastest cleanup, wash hands with soap and water immediately after handling compound, and follow directions on the package for best results.

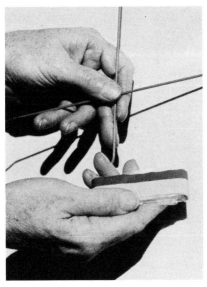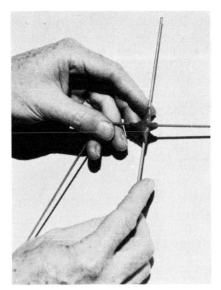

Left: a section of an epoxy ribbon (Duro's *E·pox·e Ribbon* pictured) and wires to be joined
Right: the epoxy ribbon molded around the joint

There are many epoxy products for sale at hardware stores; be sure to ask for an epoxy ribbon, such as Duro *E·pox·e Ribbon.*

TIEING PLANTS

When tieing plant stems to the wire forms, you may use string, plastic ribbons, or twist fasteners that are sold under different brand names such as *Tie-ems. Tie-ems* are the plastic or paper ties used to close bread bags and other perishables. If you prefer, you may buy at nurseries and plant shops larger *Tie-ems* that are especially designed for use with plants. These ties are better because they are stronger and will be less likely

15

to damage tender plant stems than string. In addition, their green color blends nicely with the plant.

When attaching plant stems to the wire forms, gently curve the stem to conform to the shape of the wire. Once the stems have attached themselves securely to the frame you may remove the *Tie-ems* or string. This process usually takes from three to five months.

POTS

Terra-cotta pots are recommended for plant sculptures. Lighter weight pots are not heavy enough to support the wire form and plant.

Clay pots come in a variety of sizes, from three to twenty-four inches in diameter. For most of the topiary projects in this book use a ten- or twelve-inch pot, although you can use a bigger size if your form is larger than the one pictured.

You should soak new clay pots in water for a few hours or overnight so they will not absorb the water you give the plant after potting or repotting. If you are using old clay pots, clean them thoroughly with soap and hot water to destroy any insect infestation.

You can also use other containers for topiaries, such as buckets and tubs, but clay pots look best. And, since they have porous walls, moisture will evaporate slowly, which is good for the plants.

Silhouette Topiary Projects

This chapter gives directions for making silhouette topiaries in various animal shapes. These forms, like the fish and the butterfly, are simple to make because they consist of just a single strand of wire.

After the plants are potted and the form inserted into the soil, the plant stems are tied to the form using *Tie-ems* or string. The sculpture is completed when the wire form is completely covered with leaves.

The time needed to complete a silhouette topiary depends on the type of plant used, the size of the plant when you begin, and how fast it grows. If you start with a young plant in a three-inch pot, you will need at least three to six months to complete a project. However, if you buy or have on hand a more mature plant in a five-inch pot, completion time would be from five to ten weeks.

Follow the step-by-step illustrated instructions included with each topiary, and enjoy watching your animal garden grow!

FISH

The shape of a fish adapts well to plant sculpture, and the wire form can be as small or as large as you want. A small fish topiary is charming, the larger one more dramatic. The small fish pictured here can be completed—the plants fully grown around the form—in about five to seven weeks.

DIRECTIONS FOR MAKING THE WIRE FORM

Bend a fifty-inch piece of wire into a fish shape. Join wires at the nose with an epoxy ribbon.

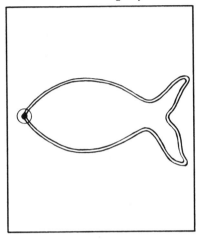

Attach two eighteen-inch support wires.

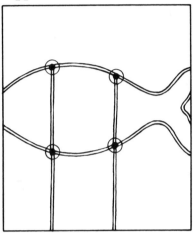

Bend a ten-inch piece of wire for the fin, and join to the other wires as shown.

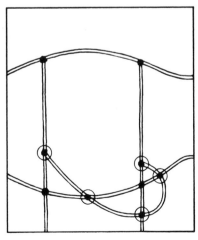

Attach a three-inch piece of wire for the fish's mouth.

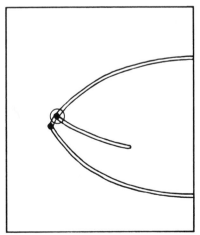

Note: ● Join with epoxy ribbon.

POTTING AND TRAINING THE PLANTS

❧ Buy two separate *Hypocyrta* plants, each planted in a three-inch pot.

❧ Repot the plants in a ten-inch pot, placing the plants four inches apart.

❧ Push the two support wires of the form firmly into the soil between the plants.

❧ When plant stems are six inches long, start tieing them to the wire with *Tie-ems* or string. As you tie the stems mold them gently to the shape of the wire. Trim any stray leaves and stems that do not conform to the wire form.

❧ As the plant continues to grow, keep removing the excess stems that branch off to the side in order to encourage more vertical growth at the top.

❧ Keep wrapping stems around the wires as the plant grows. Eventually the leaves should completely cover the form. Use a single or double strand of leaves to emphasize the outline of the fish and to create a silhouette effect when the topiary is viewed from a distance.

PLANT TIPS

Hypocyrta, popularly called the goldfish plant because its orange flowers are shaped like a fish, is a houseplant that is simple to grow indoors. The plant has small, bright-green leaves on trailing stems and is a cascading plant that can be easily trained to grow vertically.

20

The goldfish plant likes a porous soil that is kept evenly moist, never dry or too soggy. *Hypocyrta* will, if necessary, grow in shade, but it does better in bright light. Sunlight is not necessary, however.

Water plants every third day, and keep excess leaves trimmed. Occasionally wash leaves with a damp cloth to keep the plant sculpture dust free and attractive.

Hint: When buying your goldfish plants, ask for *Hypocyrta strigilosa.*

LION

This plant sculpture is somewhat larger, but is a handsome and easy one to do. The basic form of the lion is simple and the curves are gradual, so training the plant to the wire is not complicated.

DIRECTIONS FOR MAKING THE WIRE FORM

Bend a seventy-two-inch piece of wire into a lion shape, joining the wire at the foot as shown. Attach two eighteen-inch support wires.

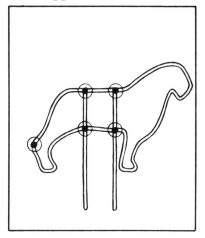

Attach a thirty-six-inch piece of wire for the tail and an eighteen-inch wire for the lion's other back leg. Join the wires as shown.

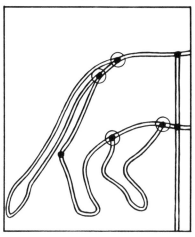

Make the lion's other front leg by attaching a twelve-inch piece of wire.

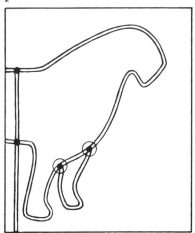

Use two six-inch wires for its ears, and attach a three-inch wire for its mouth.

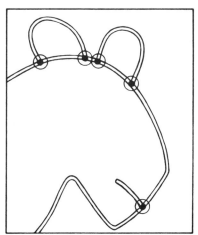

Note: ⊙ Join with epoxy ribbon.

POTTING AND TRAINING THE PLANTS

❧ Plant four small *Peperomia plants,* two on each side of a twelve-inch pot.

❧ Push the two support wires of the form firmly into the soil between the plants.

❧ Begin tieing the *Peperomia* stems to the lion form with *Tie-ems* or string when the plants are four inches tall. *Peperomia* leaves are spaced far apart, so you will have to put one stem on top of another to make a double strand and then tie the stems to the form. As you tie the stems mold them gently to the shape of the wire.

❧ As the plant grows continue to train it to the form, attaching the stems with *Tie-ems* or string.

❧ Trim any stray leaves and stems that do not conform to the shape.

PLANT TIPS

Peperomia is a popular houseplant because it does not need much water to thrive. It has small, rounded, green leaves closely set on the stems and grows easily in a porous soil. Keep the lion in the shade; in the sun *Peperomia* does not do well. The plant is a natural trailer and simple to train on wire forms because the stems are so flexible.

Hint: When buying your *Peperomia* plants, ask for trailing, small-leaved *Peperomia.*

RABBIT

The wire form of this silhouette topiary is not difficult to make, but it does require more time than the fish or the lion. The charm of this rabbit is that if properly shaped on the wire form, it will look as if it is running.

DIRECTIONS FOR MAKING THE WIRE FORM

Bend a thirty-two-inch piece of wire for the body. Join at the nose. Attach two eighteen-inch support wires.

Bend an eight-inch piece of wire into a circle for the tail. Attach a twelve-inch wire for the back leg.

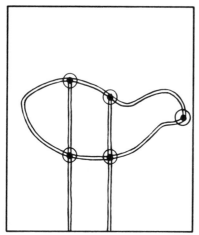

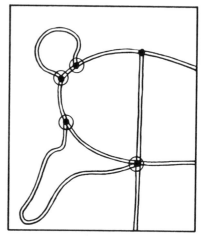

Attach a twelve-inch wire for the right front leg. Then join a nine-inch wire for the left front leg.

Attach a twelve-inch wire for one ear. Attach a nine-inch wire to the ear and the head to form the second ear.

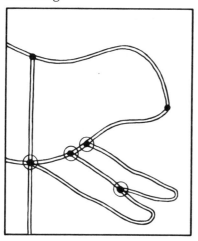

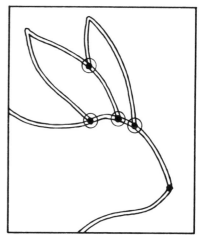

Note: ● Join with epoxy ribbon.

POTTING AND TRAINING THE PLANTS

❦ Buy two separate *Lysimachia nummularia* plants, commonly known as creeping Jenny or Charlie. Repot them in a ten-inch pot.

❦ Push the two support wires of the form firmly into the soil between the plants.

❦ When the stems are about six inches long, start tieing the stems to the wires with *Tie-ems* or string every quarter inch or so. As you tie the stems mold them gently to the shape of the wire.

❦ Double-wrap the form with stems if you have enough length after you have created a full figure.

❦ Trim any stray leaves and stems that do not conform to the shape of the wire form.

PLANT TIPS

Bright light and ample moisture will make your rabbit grow rapidly and lushly. Keep the soil evenly moist, and spray the leaves occasionally.

Hint: Lysimachia leaves grow so closely that they almost touch. You can remove some leaves if you want without hurting the plant.

SNAIL

The plant-sculpture snail, with its covering of green leaves, will add a note of whimsy to your indoor animal garden. The snail wire form has gradually curved lines and is an easy shape to work with. There are no intricate twists or turns.

DIRECTIONS FOR MAKING THE WIRE FORM

Form the snail's body by bending a thirty-two-inch piece of wire. Join the wires at tail as shown.

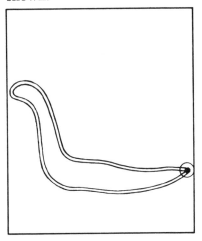

Bend its shell from a thirty-inch piece of wire.

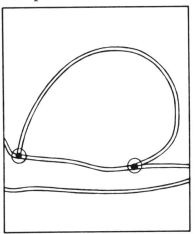

Add two eighteen-inch support wires.

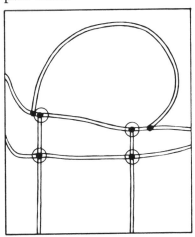

Make feelers from six-inch wires, and bend as shown.

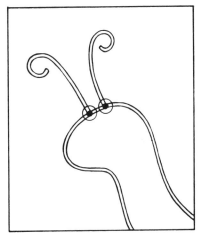

Note: ⊙ Join with epoxy ribbon.

POTTING AND TRAINING THE PLANTS

❧ Plant four small variegated ivy plants, two at the back and two in the front of a ten-inch pot.

❧ Push the two support wires of the form firmly into the soil between the plants.

❧ Start to tie the stems to the base with *Tie-ems* or string when the stems are two to four inches long. As you tie the stems mold them gently to the shape of the wire. The leaves of this ivy are spaced about one-half inch apart, so double-wrap the stems on the form to fill in the spaces.

❧ Ivy grows quickly so keep wrapping stems around the form.

❧ Trim any stray leaves and stems that do not conform to the shape of the wire form.

PLANT TIPS

Variegated ivy needs moisture and bright light. Keep leaves misted, and wash them occasionally with a damp cloth to discourage any infestation by red spider mites.

Hint: There are dozens of ivy varieties available today. The one pictured in the photograph is called Glacier. Ivy with handsome variegation in the leaves makes for a more outstanding plant sculpture.

TURTLE

Turtles make fine topiaries because all the lines are round, and plants adapt readily to this form. Besides, a turtle in the garden is fun!

For this turtle sculpture, *Ficus pumila,* or creeping fig (a member of the fig family), is used. It is a rapidly growing plant that does well indoors. The length of the turtle's wire form is somewhat longer than most of the others in this book so be certain to buy mature plants.

DIRECTIONS FOR MAKING THE WIRE FORM

Bend a thirty-six-inch piece of
wire into the shape of a turtle
shell. Join the wires as shown.

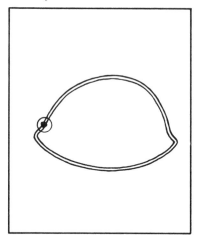

Use another thirty-six-inch
piece of wire for the body.

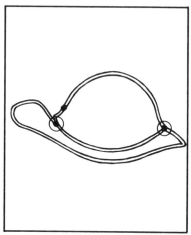

Attach two eighteen-inch support wires.

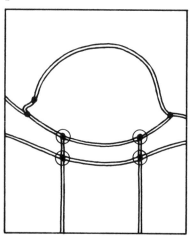

Bend two ten-inch wires into
a **U** shape for the turtle's legs.

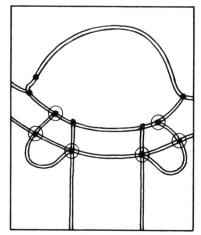

32

Note: ● Join with epoxy ribbon.

POTTING AND TRAINING THE PLANTS

❧ Carefully unwind the stems; *Ficus* stems have a way of getting tangled.

❧ Plant two plants in a ten-inch pot.

❧ Push the two support wires of the form firmly into the soil between the plants.

❧ Start to tie the stems to the base of the form with *Tie-ems* or string when they are two to four inches long. As you tie the stems mold them gently to the shape of the wire and hold them securely against it.

PLANT TIPS

Ficus is a woody plant and does not grow in a straight line. The stems are somewhat gnarled, so tight tieing is necessary. Since the leaves are set one almost on top of the other, tie them securely every one-quarter inch. Keep the plant trained to the frame. Trim any stray leaves and stems that do not conform to the shape of the wire form.

Hint: Grow *Ficus* in a bright location. Give it plenty of moisture, and mist the leaves every few days.

BUTTERFLY

Real butterflies are graceful and beautiful but always on the move and difficult to see. However, the butterfly plant sculpture you make will grace your table and be visible at all times. This ivy sculpture is a bit more difficult to make because it has more wires and curves to train the plants on. It will be necessary to trim and clip the plants more frequently to keep the shape you want.

DIRECTIONS FOR MAKING THE WIRE FORM

Bend an eight-inch piece of wire into an oval shape for the butterfly's head. To make the body, shape a twenty-inch wire into a **U** shape.

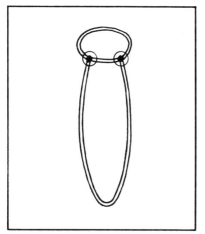

Use two thirty-inch lengths of wire for the top wings and two twenty-inch lengths for the bottom wings.

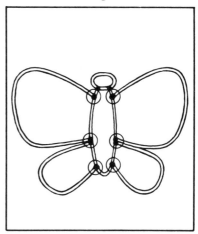

Bend two six-inch wires as shown for the antennae.

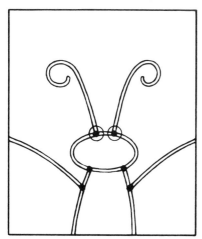

Attach two eighteen-inch support wires.

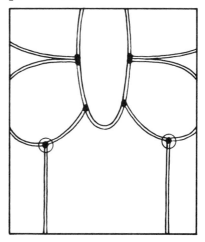

Note: ⊙ Join with epoxy ribbon.

POTTING AND TRAINING THE PLANTS

❧ Plant two miniature ivy plants in a ten-inch pot.

❧ Push the two support wires of the form firmly into the soil.

❧ When the ivy stems are two to four inches long, tie the plant stems closely to the wires with *Tie-ems* or string every one-half inch. As you tie the stems mold them gently to the shape of the wire. Do one side of the form at a time. You are basically outlining four circles.

❧ Trim any stray leaves and stems that do not conform to the butterfly shape. Because ivy has woody stems you can twist and curve it more readily than most plants.

PLANT TIPS

Ivy is a favorite houseplant, although not an easy one to grow. It requires bright light but not direct sunlight, and the soil must be evenly moist at all times. Mist the foliage frequently. Red spider mites have a fondness for ivy leaves, so if small webs appear, wash leaves with a combination of one-half bar of laundry soap (not detergent) mixed with two quarts of water.

Hint: When buying your ivy plants, ask for any of the miniature *Hedera helix* varieties.

Moss-covered Topiary Projects

The silhouette topiaries of the donkey and swan that follow are somewhat more difficult to do than the earlier silhouette projects. In this method, sphagnum moss is wrapped around the wire form, then the plants are tied to the moss-covered form using *Tie-ems* or string. The moss gives the sculptures an added fullness.

Sphagnum is a living moss that is steamed and purified before being packaged. It is sold in bags at nurseries, plant shops, and five-and-dime stores. This moss is spongy, so it holds water and dries out slowly. Thus plants attached to sphagnum moss have the advantage of a good supply of moisture at their stem. Mist the moss frequently so that the plant stems attach themselves tightly to it.

To attach sphagnum moss to the forms, tear off a piece small enough to hold in your hand. Shape the moss into a long roll. Hold the roll against the wire form, and tie it to the form with florist wire. Be sure the moss is firmly attached to the form.

DONKEY

The donkey may be a cumbersome animal in real life, but as a plant sculpture it is quite handsome. The wire form is a wide one, because of the donkey's length, so select a container that is about ten or twelve inches in diameter to achieve the correct proportion.

DIRECTIONS FOR MAKING THE WIRE FORM

Bend a fifty-inch piece of wire for the donkey's body. Join the wires at the nose as shown. Attach two eighteen-inch support wires.

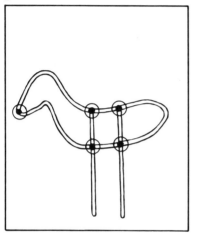

Use a twenty-four-inch wire for one rear leg and an eighteen-inch wire for the other. Attach a sixteen-inch wire for the tail.

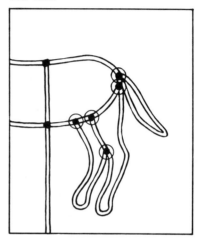

Make the donkey's front legs from two eighteen-inch pieces of wire.

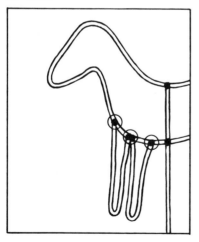

Attach two twelve-inch wires for the ears.

Note: ● Join with epoxy ribbon.

POTTING AND TRAINING THE PLANTS

❧ Plant two *Ficus pumila* plants in a ten-inch pot, one on the left and one on the right side.

❧ Push the two support wires of the form firmly into the soil between the plants.

❧ Wrap the wire form with sphagnum moss and tie it with florist wire. Make sure the form is completely covered.

❧ When the stems are from two to four inches long, begin to attach them to the moss-covered frame using *Tie-ems* or string. You will find that the woody stems of the *Ficus,* or creeping fig, are easily bent to cover the wire.

❧ As the plant grows, continue to attach stems to the form.

❧ Trim any stray leaves and stems that do not conform to the shape of the donkey.

PLANT TIPS

The creeping fig likes a soil that is evenly moist, so water it generously, but do not overwater the plant. Put the topiary in bright light, and remember to mist the moss and leaves frequently so the plant grows well.

Hint: Be sure to ask for *Ficus pumila* by its botanical name so that you will be certain to get the proper plant. Some *Ficus* plants have very large leaves, the rubber tree, for example, that would not be suitable for topiary work.

SWAN

The swan, graceful in its natural surroundings, can be just as graceful shaped in wire. The gentle curves of the swan lend itself to a handsome topiary. A good size wire form to work with is about thirty inches tall and twenty-eight inches long.

DIRECTIONS FOR MAKING THE WIRE FORM

Bend a seventy-two-inch piece of wire into the shape of a swan. Join wires at the tail as shown.

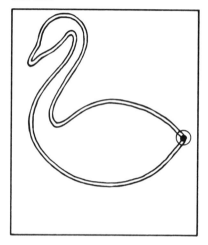

Attach two eighteen-inch support wires.

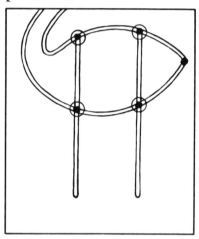

Bend wings from a twenty-eight-inch piece of wire.

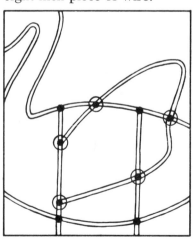

Add two wire supports as shown to strengthen the swan's long neck.

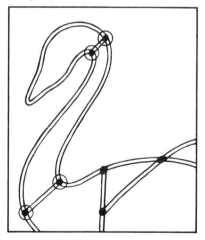

Note: ● Join with epoxy ribbon.

POTTING AND TRAINING THE PLANTS

❧ Plant four baby *Columnea* plants in a ten-inch pot.

❧ Wrap sphagnum moss around the form and tie with florist wire. Make sure the form is covered completely.

❧ Start securely tieing the plant stems to the wire with *Tie-ems* or string when they are six inches long. As you tie the stems mold them gently to the shape of the wire. When new growth occurs, keep tieing it to the form.

❧ Trim any stray leaves and stems that do not conform to the shape of the wire form.

PLANT TIPS

Columnea is a member of the gesneriad group and has tiny oval leaves closely set together on long stems. The stems are more fragile than those of ivy, so work slowly and carefully to be sure you do not break any stems. *Columnea* is a trailer or climber and likes a somewhat sandy soil that is not overly moist and prefers a shady spot. Sun and heat will hinder maximum growth, so keep the topiary in the coolest room. Also don't forget to mist the moss and foliage periodically.

Hint: The best *Columnea* for topiary work is *Columnea arguta*.

Three-dimensional Topiary Projects

After trying a few silhouette topiaries you may want to attempt a three-dimensional one. Because they have fullness and depth, these miniature topiaries are very similar to the larger outdoor ones. The forms of the three-dimensional rabbit and duck in this section have many more inner wires than those of the silhouette topiaries. Thus, the three-dimensional projects require more work, and the plants need a longer time to grow around the wires. The actual time a plant takes to cover the form depends on the kind of plant used, whether you start with a seedling or a mature plant, and how fast the plant grows.

In addition, the care of the three-dimensional topiaries is somewhat different from that of the silhouette types. Like the moss-covered silhouette projects, all of the plants used in these topiaries need frequent misting. The sphagnum moss must be kept moist so that the plant stems grow into the moss and attach themselves tightly to the form. Once they are secure, you can remove the *Tie-ems* or strings. This process usually takes from three to five months.

RABBIT

In contrast to the two-dimensional rabbit on page 25, this rabbit is three dimensional. It will make a charming accent for your desk or dresser and, unlike real-life rabbits, will not hop away. We used the plant known as creeping Jenny or Charlie (*Lysimachia nummularia*) for this topiary. A natural vining plant, it is easy to work with.

DIRECTIONS FOR MAKING THE WIRE FORM

Take two thirty-six-inch pieces of wire and one forty-eight-inch piece. Make three ovals (A). Add three twenty-inch wires around the rabbit's body (B). Attach three eight-inch support wires (C).

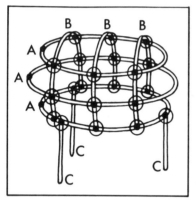

Attach a U-shaped wire for the back of the head and a ten-inch wire, bent as shown, for the front.

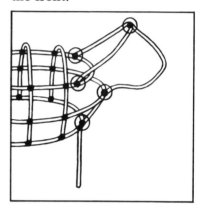

Shape two eight-inch wires for the ears. Add a U-shaped support wire at the front.

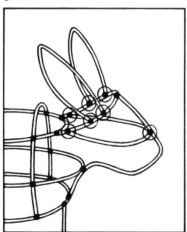

To make the tail, attach a ten-inch piece of wire to the top two oval wires as shown.

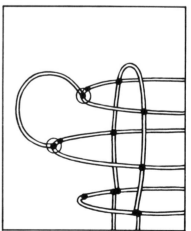

46

Note: ● Join with epoxy ribbon.

POTTING AND TRAINING THE PLANTS

❧ Plant four small *Lysimachia* plants in an eight- or ten-inch pot.

❧ Push the two support wires of the form into the soil between the plants.

❧ Wrap sphagnum moss around the wires; attach the moss with florist wire. Because there are so many wires this process will take time and patience.

❧ When the stems are two to four inches long, tie the plant stems to the moss with *Tie-ems* or string. Remember always to start from the inside and work to the outside. Train the stems as you tie them in place by gently curving them to the shape of the wire.

❧ As the plant continues to grow, remove errant stems and leaves periodically.

PLANT TIPS

Lysimachia is a handsome plant with small, round, green leaves. It is a natural trailing or cascading plant so it makes topiary work easy. The stems adapt easily to the form. The plant likes a somewhat moist soil all year so be sure to mist the rabbit frequently. *Lysimachia* grows rapidly in a bright window, but too much intense light can harm the plant.

Hint: The plant has leaves that are close together, almost overlapping. You can remove some leaves without harming the plant. Doing so will make the training easier to manage.

DUCK

A duck plant sculpture on your desk or table will brighten any room. Like the rabbit, the duck topiary takes more work and patience. You can use *Lysimachia* or any small-leaved trailing plant. Ivy will also work well.

DIRECTIONS FOR MAKING THE WIRE FORM

Take two thirty-six-inch pieces of wire and one forty-eight-inch piece. Make three ovals.

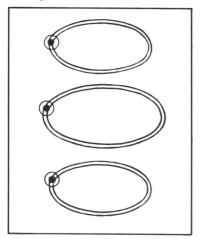

Attach three twenty-inch wires around the ovals. Add three eight-inch support wires.

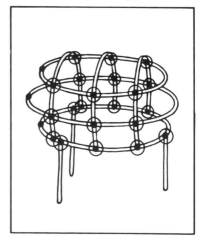

Make the duck's head from a twenty-inch piece of wire bent to the shape as shown. Attach a circular support at the duck's head as shown.

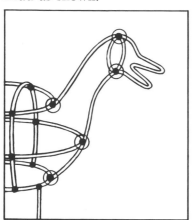

Bend a twelve-inch piece of wire for the tail. Shape a sixteen-inch wire for the wings. Add two six-inch support wires.

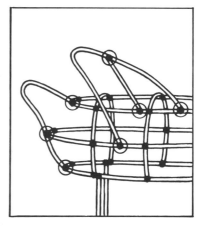

Note: ⦿ Join with epoxy ribbon.

49

POTTING AND TRAINING THE PLANTS

❦ Plant four small- to medium-sized *Lysimachia* plants in an eight- or ten-inch pot.

❦ Push the two support wires of the form firmly into the soil between the plants.

❦ Wrap sphagnum moss around the form and attach using florist wire.

❦ When the plant stems are two to four inches long, tie them to the moss with *Tie-ems* or string. Work carefully and slowly. Because there are so many wires throughout the form, remember to start from the inside and work to the outside. Train the stems as you tie them in place by gently curving them to the shape of the wire.

❦ As the plant continues to grow, remove stray leaves and stems that do not conform to the wire form.

PLANT TIPS

See pages 27 and 47 for tips on growing your *Lysimachia* plants.

Hint: When buying your plants ask for *Lysimachia nummularia,* commonly known as creeping Jenny or Charlie.

Making Your Own Pattern

This book includes instructions for making ten topiaries. After you construct a few of them, you may want to make your own pattern for a favorite animal or decorative shape. This project is not difficult to do.

Find a picture of the object you want to make in a magazine or newspaper. Place a piece of carbon paper under the picture and trace the outlines onto a sheet of white paper. Shape the wire around the outline.

If you want to make a larger topiary form, you must then enlarge the drawing. To do so, first trace the drawing onto grid paper (sold at art and variety stores). Then, using grid paper with a larger pattern, use the boxes as guides to make dots on the larger paper wherever the outline on the smaller grid drawing crosses a line. Some grid paper is ruled with both a small (¼") and a larger (1") box pattern. When all the dots have been added, connect the lines. You will have reproduced the smaller drawing in a larger size. Now use the enlarged drawing as a guide to bend and shape the wire form. Join the wires at the joints as described earlier in the book.

ENLARGING A PATTERN

Place a sheet of carbon paper between the drawing you want to copy and a piece of graph paper with a small grid pattern.

On a sheet of graph paper with a larger grid pattern, make a dot wherever a line on the smaller drawing crosses another line.

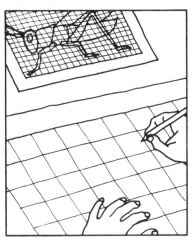

Connect the dots with a pencil.

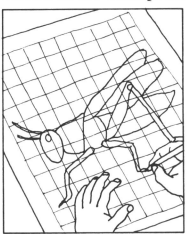

Bend the wire, using the enlarged drawing as a guide.

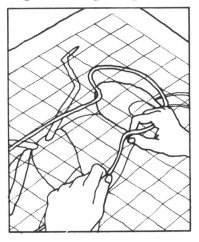

Growing and Showing Plant Sculptures

For the ten topiaries in this book several kinds of indoor plants have been used. If your topiaries are to become beautiful sculptures, you must keep your plants healthy. The information in this chapter tells you how to grow and show your topiaries, how to repot them, how to feed and water them, and how to doctor plants if insects attack them.

SOIL AND FEEDING

Plants for topiaries, like any houseplant, need a nutritional soil or they will die. The soil must be porous (have air spaces) so that water and air can move freely through it. Years ago people had to mix their own special soils for plants, but today you can buy excellent soils in handy hobby-sized sacks. The small sack, which contains one cubic yard, is enough soil for one ten- or twelve-inch pot. The three-cubic yard bag provides soil for three large pots. These packages of soil are marketed under various trade names and contain adequate nutrients for plants. Squeeze the bag to make sure it is porous. If you have some soil left over after you have potted plants, store it by securely wrapping the package and placing it in a dry, shady, cool location, like under a sink or in a closet.

Unlike houseplants, topiary plants should grow slowly, so you need not feed them packaged plant foods. (Do not worry about your plants starving; there are enough nutrients in the packaged soil to last plants for several months.) But if you are too impatient to wait for an animal topiary to assume its shape, you can hasten growth by feeding the plant with a fertilizer labeled 10-10-5. The 10-10-5 label means that the food has certain amounts of the three elements plants need: 10 percent nitrogen, 10 percent phosphorous, and 5 percent potassium, in that order. Use a pellet or granular fertilizer; sprinkle the pellets or grains on top of the soil and then water the soil. The fertilizer will react chemically with the water and become a nutritious liquid.

WATER AND WATERING

There is no need to use special water for your topiary plants. Water from the tap is fine. It is a good idea, however, to use lukewarm rather than icy-cold water, which can shock plants.

When you water your topiaries, wet the soil *thoroughly* until excess water runs out the drainage holes of the pots. Always be sure to empty the excess water from the saucer. The soil must be thoroughly moist so there are no dry air pockets. Roots reaching any dry spots will stop growing, so thorough watering ensures good plant health.

Most of the plants discussed in this book need watering every third day in the spring and summer and every fifth day in the fall and winter. Good thorough watering on this schedule will keep your plants growing happily.

Occasionally mist the plant's foliage; this care is especially important during hot weather because leaves lose water through their pores at this time. A little misting helps compensate for the heavy water loss and keeps the plants healthy.

In order to keep leaves attractive and healthy, wash them occasionally with a damp cloth.

POTTING AND REPOTTING

Potting a plant is not difficult if you work neatly and orderly. Work on a waist-high table or desk, and have all supplies at hand before you start handling the plant: broken pot pieces, soil, and containers. Place a few broken pot pieces over the drainage hole to keep the soil from running out of it. Then fill the pot with a mound of soil. Do not fill the pot to the top, or soil will spill out when you water the plant. Next, depending on the project, put two, three, or four plants in the pot, spacing the plants equally apart, and fill in around the plants with soil. Pack the soil down with your thumbs or a blunt-nosed, wooden potting stick. The soil should be firm but not tightly packed.

When the plants are firmly embedded, water the soil thoroughly. Then push the support wires of the form deeply into the soil.

Once every year dig out the top two inches of soil with a stick and replace with fresh soil. A complete re-potting of a topiary—removing the plant and form from the pot—is very difficult. It is best to crack the pot with a hammer and remove the topiary and root ball. Crumble away any old soil and trim the dead roots (those with brown tips). Then follow the potting process described earlier. It is far better to lose a pot than the topiary you have worked on for so long.

INSECTS

Sometimes, no matter how careful you are, insects will attack your plants. The first preventative against insects is to know what the common ones look like. Once you recognize the insects, you can then take steps to eliminate them so they do not kill your topiaries. The following handy reference chart of insects will help you to identify these pests.

INSECTS	HOW TO RECOGNIZE THEM
mealybugs	little insects that deposit white, cottony clusters on stems and leaves
thrips	almost invisible yellow, brown, or black insects that suck life from plants

aphids	green, black, or red oval-shaped pests about one sixteenth of an inch long
mites	tiny, hard-to-detect insects that can sometimes be seen swimming in the water for a few seconds during plant watering
white flies	resemble small mosquitoes
red spider	little spiders that leave telltale webs
scale	oval-shaped insects with hard or soft shells about one eighth of an inch long

PREVENTATIVES

Now that you know what harmful plant insects look like, what do you do if you see them? At the first sign of these pests, vigorously spray soapy water (not a detergent) on plants, and then rinse plants with clear water. To eliminate aphids, thoroughly wash the plant in the sink or brush the aphids with a solution of one tablespoon of alcohol dissolved in one quart of soapy water. A mixture of laundry soap and water deters red spiders, and mealybugs can be killed with a dab of pure alcohol. Scale is hard to eliminate, but a remedy that often works is to soak old cigarette tobacco in water for a few days and then apply the mixture with a toothbrush directly to the scale.

TRIMMING AND GROOMING

In order to keep your topiaries attractive looking, you

must occasionally trim off stray leaves and stems as the plants continue to grow.

To trim properly, stand several feet away from the sculpture. You will immediately see any leaves and stems that do not conform to the wire shapes. For example, a rabbit figure with stray stems or leaves on its back is easy to spot. Cut off these straggly pieces with a sterile knife. (Pass the knife through a match flame to make it sterile.) Or use manicure scissors for cutting. (Always be careful when using cutting instruments.)

Cutting away plant leaves and stems does not hurt the plant and will keep the topiary figure looking well groomed. No one wants to display a straggly duck or a poorly formed butterfly.

an attractive display of indoor topiaries

DISPLAYING INDOOR TOPIARIES

How you display your topiaries is up to you, of course. Since each one is distinctive you may want to choose a place in your room where you can show it off to best advantage by itself. Or you may want to combine it in a group with other plant sculptures.

Placed on a windowsill or on top of a table or desk near a window, your topiaries will get the light they need for maximum growth. With the proper care and attention your plant sculptures will bring you years of enjoyment.

Mail Order Suppliers

PLANTS

Alberts & Merkel Bros., Inc.
P. O. Box 537
Boynton Beach, Florida 33435

Arthur Eames Allgrove
Box 459
Wilmington, Massachusetts 01887

Buell's Greenhouses
Eastford, Connecticut 06242

Fischer Greenhouses
Linwood, New Jersey 08221

Henrietta's Nursery
1345 North Brawley
Fresno, California 93705

Margaret Ilgenfritz Orchids
Box 665
Monroe, Michigan 48161

Kartuz Greenhouses
92 Chestnut Street
Wilmington, Massachusetts 01887

Logees Greenhouses
55 North Street
Danielson, Connecticut 06239

Merry Gardens
Camden, Maine 04843

Oak Hill Gardens
P. O. Box 25, Binnie Road
West Dundee, Illinois 60118

DURO'S *E·POX·E RIBBON*

Woodhill/Permatex, Inc.
P. O. Box 7183
Cleveland, Ohio 44128

Topiary Plants

Columnea arguta

Ficus pumila, or creeping fig

Hedera helix, needlepoint ivy

Hedera helix, variegated ivy

Hypocyrta strigilosa,
or goldfish plant

Lysimachia nummularia,
or creeping Jenny or Charlie

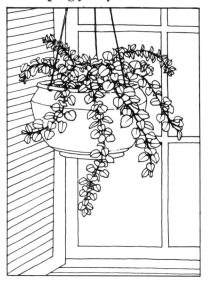

Peperomia glomerata

Schizocentron, or Spanish shawl

About the Author

Jack Kramer was born in Chicago and educated at the University of Illinois in Urbana. He has been a full-time writer since 1965 and has had over sixty books published. A member of the Garden Writers Association of America, Mr. Kramer has appeared on national television and writes a syndicated column for the *Los Angeles Times Syndicate*. He presently lives in Mill Valley, California.